FOR THE RAISED CONSCIOUSNESS OF THE NEW ERA

Commanding The Spirits Within

ANUNNAKI PSYCHIC SPIRIT FAIRIE

Kaciana Bru

DEDICATION

This book is a dedication to The Great Omnipotent Creative Substance who does declare a thing and it is.

To my twin flame, and true love G.H.J.R. the Anunnaki King from Sirius. Your Heavenly Guidance provided every word. Thank you for your patience, your love, and your dedication. IAM grateful.

We shall truly be together again.

Table of Contents

ACKNOWLEDGMENTS

Thank you Terrence, Chante, Ariana you are the High Priest, and Priestesses that my soul loves. Be Blessed At All Times.

Praise The Most High Omnipotent Source.

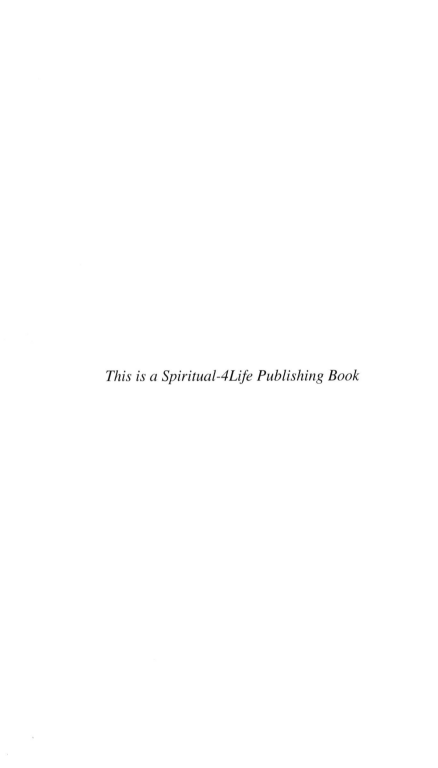

This is a Spiritual-4Life Publishing Book

FOR THE

RAISED CONSCIOUSNESS

OF THE NEW ERA

Within this writing is channeled information from Anunnaki energy.

THE INVOCATION

May the Highest Great Creative Source of All grant that my experiences be my greatest achievements delivered to me by Universal Source Energy. As I receive all good things in abundance I shall let go and trust. I shall trust and let go.

Intention

The intention is that everyone who reads this book will realize some subtle facts. That the intelligent thinker we call the subconscious is a spirit that wants to see you win, a close companion, a best friend, and a distinct and separate personality.

Begin no task without announcing to the universe your declared intention over it. The intention process is a crucial step in all that you do, start nothing without it. The intention you place on a thing will help to enhance its activity. Your intention is a witness for your hearts desires, and is your expressed desire to fulfill your will. Every intention is a gift you offer to the Universe. Wear your intention as an emblem. Announce your intent to all that you meet. The happiness these announcements bring will help you receive quickly.

There is a powerful spirit within everyone listening for a command. The spiritual power is your subconscious mind and acts on your firm genuine intention. This spiritual force is directing interior energies to help meet and receive your exterior objectives.

Inherently you have the power to choose to use the help of the spirits within your vessel in contrast to your earthly friends. This powerful spiritual energy within your vessel is a gift from universal energy. This Omnipotent Universal Mind is listening and will never try to force you to do or be any thing.

The Great Universal Force that put you on earth truly loves you. This Great Creative Consciousness takes care of you, and truly never sleeps. Provisions, opportunities, and much help for success are yours to achieve. You did nothing to receive the gifts and no one can take them away. These gifts are with you until the end.

The heavenly energy that resides within you has led you here to gain some particular insight(s) that your soul needs to hear. Did you think the power to hear is yours for the purpose of enjoyment? No. The hearing is given to you so that when you return home, from the earthly realm, you will be happy and at peace.

This book expects to inspire everyone that reads it to receive his or her greatest increase. We want you to know that it is possible for you to quickly hear the guides within you and command those guides accordingly.

Opening

May the contents of this book be spread

everywhere across the globe. May every living person that hears the words within implement the principles. May this book be a blessing to all through eternity.

Intended "For the Raised Consciousness of The New Era." There will come a time when everyone will consciously hear his or her inner guidance. The contents of this book are useable applications until everyone across the globe is listening.

The contents of this book have been received directly through spiritual realms as psychic experiences and from my spirit guide G.H.J.R. the Anunnaki. The title of this book was delivered by spirit guides during a dream state, wherein I was told to get up and write. The techniques within are unique, and in an easy to understand format.

Within the book, you are given the tools to speak with your inner guides who possess the ability to bless you at every turn. You have been fully equipped to win. After reading this book if you do anything other than win, there will be no opportunity for you to blame any energy and/or spirit other than your own.

There are earthly powers that have a duty to make sure you continue going around in circles, recycling and populating the land. You spend your entire life giving the earthly realm all your energy, and then die without taking any of it with you. Ask yourself, if we do not get to keep any of those things we created why come back? We return to earth without any memory and have to start many things over again, our energy is bound to the earth. God has given you all the necessary tools so that you do not have to come back to earth.

You must get yourself spiritually connected to the universal source energy to get the proper training because schools of so called "education" are not teaching the information. Usually by the time you decipher all information needed to win your ascension, your time on earth is almost up, and you will need to come back.

Those thoughts and memories connected to

our heart center will always stay with us. These things include our in-built skills, and the inherent love that our actions have wrought. If earth is fantastic, imagine how much more wonderful heaven is, compared to earth?

There is truly an awakening happening on earth. I am proof of it. Soon we will all hear our spirit guides. I thought hearing voices was wrong and every time I heard a spirit open its mouth it was told to shut up. Not anymore, I am grateful for their help. IAM truly listening to spirit guides from heavenly realms.

Your thoughts are powerful.

Thoughts can take any experience and change it into a living hell, or an extravagant heaven. Give thanks.

ARISING TO A NEW
CONSCIOUSNESS

It is impermissible to have disturbances and outbreaks in heaven. Life Universal knows everything about you. It is because of this that the growth and expansion of your soul is the designated cosmic goal. Change and adapt with each opportunity for growth, and you will receive a fuller version of yourself.

Great Creative Substance has assigned mandatory accomplishments for your soul that are in direct relationship to the golden thread of all your past experiences. It is important to note that these appointed assignments are fixed; your energy directs the outcome through choices. You will continue growing, so that your undergo a continuous development.

You will never be able to blame Source Energy for anything. Additionally, it will not take all eternity for the completion of your mission. Hence you have no control over the heartbeat within you. Also, as others complete their missions, circumstances will change. Therefore, you will recycle as necessary to complete your heavenly goal. Neither you, nor time is in control of your destiny.

Everything on the planet is, one big dream, a measure of someone's thought. Within this thought filled habitat you are given the opportunity to leave your thoughts behind and live in the future through the moment of now. Every thought is a prayer. This in itself tells us that we are powerless over the great creative substance.

Creative Thought

Where do thoughts come from? After all,

we do not even have the ability to control the beats within the body or vessel that we are a part. No one has power to control the receipt, and luxury of eyesight, and the power does not belong to us to give the mind a thought. It is evident that thoughts do not come from us.

Why were we created to become a part of an experience that is not really, real? Someone is always dreaming and creating with their mind. It is impossible for Creative Substance to come up with small thoughts. You will know when you have connected to creative substance because you will have bigger thoughts than you ever dreamed.

Here are some ways to become closer to creative substance.

- Connect yourself to the interests that you had during your young age. What did you like to do when you were a child? This will probably be the path that you should follow.
- Follow your passion.
- Quiet your mind, find the center of your

vessel, and communicate with the inner you.

- Take care to daily send messages of your goals and intentions to Creative Source which always hears your thoughts.

- You will begin to hear source energy communicating with you.

Every imagined thought in the earthly realm starts out as a fantasy. Your unique vibration mixes with the creative substance of the universe and this connection makes you the master of the Earth and a friend of all its realms. Your desires help create your vibration. Every fantasized dream is a creation that has manifested into a vibratory form.

The created physical form on earth is full of people's dreams, hopes, and aspirations. In all spaces that you shall look you shall find a reflection of someone's thought. On earth most thoughts are recycled and copied. Everything has always been in existence naturally so you may create. Each individual thought you are given is a means to help you grow.

At all times you are making the right decision and life gets easier when you realize there are no wrong or right results for any occurrence. An occurrence is only something that happens. Every choice is a learning experience, and all experiences are good for the soul.

There is an inborn non-conscious thought process that drove us up the womb of our mother, and into the egg of life. From the Great Creative Substance we were born into a world of dreams and illusions already created before we arrived. No one wants to naturally make the wrong decisions in life. There has been given to us an imbedded thought pattern to win this time, and it is lodged within each soul.

Spiritual Guides Are Always With You

The spiritual realm sends you every thought. Hearing voices means your spiritual guides are with you. Many of us have heard people tell others to be cautious if someone starts talking to him/herself quietly or aloud. Do not listen to those that tell you not to talk aloud or that hearing voices is crazy, it is not. Additionally, hearing voices and talking aloud is a gift that will help you command the spirits within.

The truth is you are to master the voices, and thoughts within. Tell yourself you will win against those entities that warn you against using your natural gifts. You will win against the powers that want to keep you tied to an existence that is not real. The only thing that is real is love, and what happens from within.

One of the most powerful tools you have is the spoken word. Words are powerful and you should speak them aloud at each available opportunity. That means talk to yourself constantly.

Your Life Mission

Every soul comes to the earthly realm to complete a mission, and like all missions, this assignment requires a time limitation. Consider your heartbeat the clock. Your souls past accomplishments and future goals determine your soul mission. Everyone will return to their original substance, organized by the Great Creative Substance which bore it from the beginning. This is a great divine plan, which no man can change.

The earthly sojourn you take has been pre-declared for you. It is not a decision you can rethink. Your life path is already set. Your path is a thing declared for you, before you took possession of the human form. It does not matter what choice you make as to who your master will be. It also, does not matter whom you choose to serve. Your complete journey from the beginning is in the heavenly records and shows what course you will take.

1. This record is written so that you may receive help.

2. This record is complete and will not allow anyone to place blame.

3. This record is made available to your helpers for their review.

4. This record will be used for future blueprints to guide you through.

Your life is an opportunity for you to make right decisions that will bring you to your highest destiny. You do not have the ability to change it only we do. However, you do have the ability, and the great opportunity to make decisions along the way. The decisions you make help create your future reality. This reality continues in many different dimensions simultaneously.

Your success will depend on these few directives. Believe in yourself. Believe that a source higher than you exists. Believe that you receive everything from this higher source. Believe that you are living the dream, and believe it, before that which you are dreaming of is received.

Faith, belief, trust are spirits with separate and distinct personalities sent to help you. Pray that they will join you and then you will find them as your friend.

- **Faith** does not have to see what you believe.
- **Believing** is a form of hope, and means that this thing is possible.
- **Trust** is telling yourself that everything you believe for actually exists, and is available.

How To Have Faith

Be faithful in all things and you will never be afraid. When you believe and have trust, it is easy to have faith. Faith means that you do not have to see anything in this world of illusions to know that it is real. You believe it exists, before you ask.

Be faithful the Anunnaki way faith is not the same as trust. Faith is the belief that all you hoped for will arrive. You will believe that all you ask for will be received, before you receive it.

- Your voice is heard when you are sincere.
- Tell God that you know he hears you.
- Tell God that because he hears, you know that your request is delivered before you

receive.

Keep telling yourself that the creative substance that created you hears you.

- Your request is heard when you are sincere.

    1. Hear yourself as you ask for your desire.

    2. Feel the spirit of the desire go forth from you into universal energy.

    3. Tell your self that you know the thing you ask for is real, in the same manner that you are real.

You must have faith that God will do what you have requested.

Tell yourself that first you will see a thing spiritually and nothing needs to be seen before it is received on the earthly realm. Tell yourself you must believe to see it, and not the other way around. Tell yourself that the earthly realm is not real anyway because it is full of everyone's dreams. Because earth is not the reality, then your creator must be the reality. Since you cannot see your creator, but you know that it exists, in the same manner, you cannot see your blessings but you know that they exist.

How To Believe

You must believe that all things are possible. Not believe that all things are possible for your neighbor, celebrities, or those that may already have it all. Truly, believe that all things are possible for you.

Tell yourself to believe. Do you want to know how to believe in yourself? We understand that sometimes it is not easy. Sometimes, environments will tell you that it is not possible to get this or that. Do not believe it!

- Have confidence.

Allow yourself the confidence to believe in your future self. Your belief is usually much stronger after you have received. This is the reason why rich people find it easier to receive.

Nothing happens by accident, be joyful, because now we will teach you how to believe in yourself. It may not be easy. You will need to erase all of the programming previously written on the computer program of your mind.

Your creator wants you to receive. In receiving you have proof of what you have believed for.

How To Trust

You will start trusting Universal Source when you start asking for their mercy, and help. Then you will trust God. If you do not know how to trust start by conveying your gratefulness at every moment.

- Tell God that you will trust, and believe that what he wants is what you want.
- Tell God that you want to start today, trusting, and believing in him.
- That you want to start believing today there is no greater power than the power of the

Great Universal Creative Substance.

He will give you what you ask for. God loves you, and so do we. Trust the Anunnaki Way. Trust is not the same as faith. Trust believes that God will do what he said he would do. After you ask you, will:

- Truly, trust that God heard you.
- Tell God that you trust in him absolutely.
- Your request is already fulfilled tell God that you realize this to be a fact. Let God know that you have concluded the spiritual realm is the first realm in which you receive. That it is the spiritual realm that is the most important realm of all.
- Truly trust God, and then you will get all that you ask.
- Trust that God knows exactly what you want.
- Keep asking until you truly trust. This must be ongoing, so that you will have faith.

If you are having difficulty trusting God say this prayer:

> "Heavenly Creator, I will trust your help. I will trust the word that I receive from you. I will trust your heavenly Angels. I will trust you Father with all that is within me. Thank you father for helping me. Thank you father for your mercy. Thank you father for everything. I love you with all that is within me."

You will make your request known to God. Your voice will be heard when you are sincere. When you make a request the answer is available for you immediately because the Universe heard you before your mouth asked. In so doing, after you receive your request, you will prove to yourself that God is real.

Illusions

What is an illusion? Everything in the earthly realm is illusion, except love. Love is the only non-illusion there is. An illusion can be anything, and is always something that in time will disappear. The deception of time supports all other false ideas of what is real. Time is the key to the big deception. It is time that helps us wrongly perceive occurrences presented to our senses. Time is a clever trick that supports all of the illusions.

For a very long time I fought against the psychic phenomena that was happening within me. I did everything I could to forget it, and in many instances I succeeded at the task. My spiritual guidance tried everything they could to bring me back and listen to them. However, I was not having it, and I truly was not listening. Refusing to listen I made the same mistake over, and over again.

My life was not enhanced, but limited when I refused to listen and acknowledge my natural spiritual gifts. Spiritual guidance had an alternative way of teaching me that my destiny would not elude me. Strange phenomena started to occur. Things that were not supposed to be real, such as icons on a page moving, or reflections in a glass starting to take shape and these things were happening continuously.

Probably, everyone has heard of that social site called face book that wants everyone to be hooked. I was one of those facehookers. I spent, numerous wasting hours, upon hours playing games, and other tasks. Until, I woke up one day feeling as though I was one of those little moving moppets in restaurant city. OMG, I said to myself, I am spending time on this game as though it is real, and now I have embedded myself in it. Immediately, I made a promise to the Universe that I shall not permit earthly things to capture my mind completely. I will be free.

Illusions are real only in that they help you experience. You keep every experience that connects to your heart and take it back to your heavenly home with the creator. You will tell the creator which of these experiences were important to you, and which of the experiences you cared for the most. It will be effortless for you to reconnect to those things, which makes your soul prosperously happy.

You must be completely happy when you return home to your creator. It was you that left the creators kingdom in the first place and your reason was to experience. When you return you must be fully satisfied, completely happy and without disruptive attachments. There is nothing negative in the Kingdom everything is positive. Of course, there are two kingdoms; we are not talking about that now.

How To Dissolve Illusions

Anything that opposes you is an illusion and is put there as a challenge. When you want to dissolve an illusion, you simply tell it that it is not real.

Say:

"You are not real."

- You must be firm so that it will believe you.
- The illusion will disappear once you are sincere

in telling it to do so.

- Replace the unwanted illusion with its opposite polarity if necessary.

If you are or weak or the illusion believes that you are not sure of what you are saying, the illusion will not believe you. If the illusion does not believe you, it will try to teach you a lesson and come back bigger and with more fierceness.

In getting bigger, the illusion is telling you to stop lying to yourself. Listen and change your behavior so that you will receive the best results. Your goal should always be the receipt of those things that you concentrate on creatively, and since everything but love is an illusion you can make anything happen.

You will certainly meet with opposing spirits which are there to help you change direction, and help you remove obstacles that you would not ordinarily care to remove. Adhering and adapting to the helpful messages sent by spirits and listening to them are necessary.

*I don't care about faces, personalities or clothes
only the vibratory energy of the soul.*

-- G.H.J.R. The Anunnaki

AUTHENTICITY

Most of us copy the thoughts of something, or someone else. Most thoughts are absent from authenticity and are precluded from the majority of human perceptibility because of no connection and/or communication with the spiritual realm guardians, guides, or the true self.

Dependence to the earthly realm takes away some of the power to be authentic. Every earthly association takes away some of your ability to concentrate on things that create authenticity. The power to be authentic is purely dependent on spirituality and is a vibratory energy. A vibratory spiritual connection will create your authenticity.

Authentic thoughts are proof that you have connected with spirit. Unlike thoughts that have already permeated the earth, authentic thoughts are highly rewarded on the earthly realm because they are different from the norm and are considered genius or extremely unique.

Do not tell yourself there are no authentic thoughts available. The abundant universe is unlimited. The Great Creative Source has designed millions upon billions of authentic fingerprints in much the same manner that it will deliver to you your authenticity.

Authenticity is used to boost the consciousness of humanity. We can genuinely rely on authenticity to propel ourselves, but this is not easy to garner. The spirit realms and other dimensions choose individuals and vessels that will make the best use of their energy. According to that vessel capability to realize original authentic thought forms through pure universal energy the assignment shall be accomplished.

The only true reality is the Great Creative Substance. It is from this spectacular divine consciousness that we get our inner energy to create. Universal energy compounds the vibratory energy into a substance called "we." The "we" energy is the collective intelligence. This shared information has access to all pieces of knowledge capable of influencing the earthly realm.

This vibratory energy called "we" is available to anyone that is willing to connect through non-judgmental means. Everyone has access to the energy. However, all are not carriers of it. Most people do not harvest the necessary concentrated effort to garnish the "we" energy. Success belongs to carriers of this authentic "we" energy.

We receive original thought from universal energy as a gift that propels us to pioneer undiscovered territories. The fulfillment of new and innovative thoughts are formed by pure universal energy. The person, energy, or vessel that receives authentic thought leaves a strong impression on the earthly realm. Spirit never wastes its own energy and authenticity is so unique it wont be disregarded.

Spirit chooses the vessel that carries authentic thought carefully. The purpose of the authentic thought is to feed the masses and its accomplishment must be achieved.

In being different, looking different and creating new trends you are authentic. Authenticity is the creation of different and unique thoughts. The authentic thought either helps you to understand the same information in an unusual way or provides you with the potential to experience events not previously made available within its same dimension.

Alternatively, it will always be a different way of understanding. Either way the different ways of understanding allow you access to information that previously eluded you.

Vibratory Energy

Everything happens first from inside of your vessel. Example, we have two men, one is literally blind, and the other has perfect sight. The one with perfect sight can see the color of the flowers, and the blind man sees nothing but darkness. Then the angels, spirits or guides receive permission that this blind man should see, and therefore gives him sight. Naturally his vessel did not allow him the opportunity to see the color of the flowers. Nevertheless, now his inner faculties have been unblocked and he sees it all.

He experiences from within his vessel first. If the vessel is blocked he receives nothing. What happens on the inside of the body/vessel directs what is happening on the outside. The power for this to happen belongs to nothing within the earthly realm. Scientifically we acknowledge that each human thought produces a magnetic vibration. Magnetics links everything consciously, or unconsciously. With this authentic energy, there is the opportunity to experience, observe, and receive.

The Omnipotent Source cares about your pure vibration. It is not your words but the vibration of your heart that the higher spiritual energies hear. Universal energy has no favorites. The Universe does not care that you are taking out the garbage or that you are a teacher at the university. Your doings are your business and you are simply experiencing. Universal energy will step in to help when necessary. This energy is listening to vibration, and loves everyone that matches its intensity. Control your vibrations before you ask the creator for anything. The exchange of your pure vibration is how Great Creative Substance participates with you. The words that you utter are for your own use, they are alive, and are a helper to you.

The clearest strongest vibratory signal sent out from any particular vessel and with the strongest intensity and authority is heard above others.

- Find your vibration through meditation, yoga, or breathing exercises.

- Feel your vibration and love it.

You must connect to the spiritual realm to receive. Moreover, how do you make the connection? You must connect the passion of who you are with the sincere desire of the universe to support your passion through the consciousness of the "we". You must want it with all that is within you, and you must want it with joy.

Tell yourself to focus on those things that are spiritual before you receive. When earthly connections consume your mental focus spiritual energies can deplete themselves, if allowed. It will be necessary for you to replenish your spiritual energy. Let nothing stop you. Make up your mind that this thing is something you truly want.

The earthly realm is constantly trying to diminish or take away some of the vibratory energy that belongs to the spiritual realm. Care should be taken to strengthen your spiritual energy because the guarantee to minimize any or all of your weaknesses is left up to you. Your weakness will not help you, but will cause you to lag in your getting. Control your vibrations before you ask the creator for gifts. Weak gifts will not help your cause.

You will meet again that same energetic spirit you sent out before you. Energy goes out before you, and returns from behind you with the same force or greater in which you sent it. You will meet again, one day, the same spirit of vibration you send. The spirit of mercy is always available to aid you. Believe it because it is the truth. Stay completely focused on your dream.

Steps to Becoming Authentic

To the benefit of all there is the ability to create authentic thoughts. The truth is every formularized reality is a benefit to your self, and will benefit others in need.

Everything that is authentic will in turn create unimagined galaxies and occurrences first within that vessel that experienced the new and authentic thought and then for those surrounding.

Then that one authentic thought will create new worlds of possibilities as a benefit to all.

The responsibility of those that will carry authentic thought is great. You must do with the authentic thought that which spirit entrusts to you. Thoughts do not belong to you. The Great Creative Substance gives thoughts to you, and delivers them to you through spirit. Only those that are subservient to authenticity will continue to receive authentic thoughts from dimensions unknown. The spiritual universe knows, sees, and hears everything. They know who will use their authentic thought in the manner prescribed.

- No one was born with your energy.

- It is unique to you.

- Use this energy. It is your power.

- Universal Consciousness gives energy to the earth a gift.

Tell yourself that you cannot fail. Do not be afraid

to be fearless. There can never, and will never, be another you.

You cannot fail. Go anywhere, and everywhere you will go, own it!

Synchronicity

Synchronicity is a method used by the spiritual realms to point you in the right direction. Synchronicity is a spirit, and you must be spiritually alert to notice the simultaneous events. Symbols are usually the mode of communication used by the spirit of synchronicity. Those of us whom have heard of synchronicity know that it happens when an occurrence that seems totally disconnected and or coincidental captures your attention.

You cannot ignore the random, and repeated occurrences brought to you through its symbolism. These messages are from spirit. When you step out of the present moment, you step out of alignment with synchronicity. Listening to the spirit of synchronicity will help you win this time and this spirit needs you to take action in the "now."

Living in the present moment will decrease the possibility of becoming lost in the movement of endless thoughts. You have consistently received spiritual guidance from the beginning of your existence and it is a true helper. Living in the present moment and listening to your guidance will give you the opportunity to win this time.

Living In The Moment

Living in the present moment allows you to stay focused on moments that are happening now. Staying focused on what is happening now will not allow the negatives of fear, or other insecurities to develop. Because, in the now "I must do now, I must be now, and now I must act." Now is active and every moment of now propels you to your next moment of bliss.

Human thoughts produce the emotions. The present moment wants you to get it done now. Living in the now will help keep you focused on what is actually happening in the moment. Allowing you to act, and relax in each moment, and each minute of the glorious now.

Reality

Experiences are choices; the reality is that thought creates everything. Every moment you are deciding which choice to take next, and every choice you choose will create another choice. This opportunistic method of receiving is a beneficent gift from the universe. This gift is a love that supports, and makes allowances of more than enough, for everyone.

We are all connected. It may seem to you that the rich mogul whom did not share his wealth with you was stingy and, or greedy. That rich mogul gave something to humanity in return for those riches received. Take a closer look at that person and his or her deeds. Guaranteed he or she left you something by which you, or someone after you, may use for this journey.

Your perceptions do not always show you things with clarity. Universal energy is very careful to ensure that everything happens for the good of all.

Everyone has the same number of hours in their day. The person that receives the most is the one whom orchestrates their time in the wisest manner and with the highest form of power. The universe is listening for intense sincerity and the highest vibration wins. Study and show yourself approved. Raise your vibration.

Perceptions

In each thought there is a lesson. We have minds that can conceive anything. Be assured every eye that you meet has a thought accompanied by Universal Energy directed specifically for you.

All physical form is made of a dream and since everything is a dream there truly is no reality. The perception of reality changes only to help and benefit those in need. When the imagined reality is no longer useful it eventually disappears into Universal Energy.

Do you think that you do it alone? Think

again, for it was not possible for you to bring yourself in to the earthly realm. Your heartbeat has been measured and you hold no control. You will surely be on time when you leave this place and until then everything is allowed. The conscious mind accepts the totality of feelings, actions, and thoughts to be connected simultaneously. This mind and/or the spirits which guide it are constantly communicating to the true self within. Use your power and win.

Everything has a purpose. Stars are not only balls of hydrogen, they are watching for your return.

-- G.H.J.R. The Anunnaki

INCLINATIONS OF THE SPIRIT

The Witnesses

Be faithful, you are always being watched, and listened to constantly. Your spiritual guidance is listening to you all the time you are never alone. There are witnesses outside of us, and there are witnesses inside of us. These witnesses are spirits with distinct and separate personalities. You may call them watchers if you choose. These witnesses are doing much more than just watching, they are experiencing. Some of these witnesses will be standing by your side when you return to your creator. There are many witnesses and those that we describe in this chapter are connected to the actions of your subconscious mind.

The heavenly energies surrounding you do not tire. Be not dismayed there is a system put into place to ensure protection to yourself, and others against undeserved incidents. Whether or not you or someone else brought about the occurrence causing it to manifest does not matter. There are laws and protectors.

What Is Spirit

Spirit connects to the heart center. Your spirit is not inside your body. Your spirit abides around the physical body, usually hovering above the body, at all times. Your spirit stays connected to your body at all times. However, it can become damaged and weak, and has the ability to travel.

The process of thinking and the objects of all your perceptions help to form what is located within the spirit.

- Spirit is the observer in you.
- Spirit is observing everything you do.

- Spirit processes each observation.

- Your spirit caters to the true you.

- The spirit is the observer who is always doing the observing.

The spirit is where your personality resides. Your spirit listens to the true you, and becomes the essence of that which will help your true self complete its mission. You may speak to your spirit the same as you would any other spirit, like a friend. Your spirit is your distinct personality that you present to the world.

Speak to your spirit with a high amount of respect and treat it like a dignitary. Your spirit is extremely intelligent ask your spirit to seek right direction. Do not consistently badger your spirit about anything, say what you need to, and drop it. Your spirit is a witness to all that you do. You have many witnesses; your shadow is a witness too. Everything that has a shadow has a spirit.

Inward and Outer Desires

The Inward and Outward Desires of the Spirit are the desires of the true self, and the ego. Until you become acquainted with your spirit through prayer, meditation or some other tool, you must listen closely to the intent of your heart to collect its wisdom.

The inward inclination has the most power over the totality of your entire being. It is the spiritual essence of your true self.

- The inward desires are the higher desires.
- These desires are unseen, and at first seem to be quiet.

Before you are able to hear your inward spirit, and use it to your advantage, you must believe that it is there. The message from your inward spirit will become more prevalent than your outward desires when you believe it exists. You must seek the inward desires, by listening closely to the intent of your heart, to draw them out.

The outward inclinations of the spirit are the lower desires, some of which animals share with humans. They are the predatory desires, the desire to preserve the body. (i.e. eating, procreation, supremacy, etc.) These outward desires are always available and shared with the earthly realm of which you are grounded.

These outward inclinations are not necessarily negative they sometimes allow us to dominate, stand for justice, and stand for truth at the most crucial times.

- The outward desires are loud.
- The outward desires are constantly screaming thoughts at you.
- The outward desires are always demanding.

When you have purified the lower aspect or desires. The ego portion of your being is weakened. Success is then made available through the focus of your heart.

The Observer

The spirit is in the entire activity of all processes of observation. At every moment, the spirit is all observing. Spirit is the one who wants to know why you do, what you do. Spirit is the energy of the observer in you. The spirit is the creational part of you an all-registering natural spiritual awareness that is all-observing.

- The spirit observes all your ideas and activities.
- Appears behind all of your considerations.
- Holds all of your inner characteristics.

Thus, the human should always be conscious of what is spiritual, without which he/she would not be able to draw a breath, could not grasp a consciousness-based thought, recognize, see, hear, or experience anything.

I am sure you have heard people say "wow that made the hairs stand up on the back of my neck." In all your doing make the hairs stand up on the back of your neck. Make sure all that you do vibrates at a high frequency of positivity. This vibratory strength will help you succeed. With all that you do, do it with all the passion that is within you. If there is no passion it is wasted energy.

Put your self in the company of positive influences. This will help you expand your spiritual vibratory frequency within your self, and your personal space. On the other hand, controversy, and negativity will stagnate you, and this will weaken your spiritual energy.

Déjà Vu

Let us look at déjà vu this is a spirit with a distinct and separate personality that comes to remind you of past experiences. Déjà vu says, "this happened before" and with that thought we are prompted to remember.

Who hasn't experienced déjà vu? Almost everyone I know, and everyone I have asked says that they have experienced déjà vu. Well then, if so many have experienced it, we shall not call it myth, but truth.

Who is sending the déjà vu messages that give you a feeling of already experiencing the past situation, of the present moment? How, can this thought of the past be in the present awareness? Where does the thought come from?

We come to realize that within the deepest recesses of the mind we did not send that message to ourselves. The reason why déjà vu is such a phenomenon is because confusion surmounts after having felt the experience of the past in this future moment. It is usually too complicated to comprehend that somehow this present thought has already been experienced in a time that has passed and cannot be remembered.

We store the thought away in our memory banks, because we cannot solve it. The thought is stored to resurface again in some other future moment of time. This future moment of time sometimes recreates itself over, and over again in the earthly realm. Time only exists in the mind.

The message that accompanies déjà vu is a wakeup call and an opportunity to change the outcome of this present situation. When the spirit of déjà vu shows up you must act immediately, and usually you only have seconds to respond before it disappears.

Listen to your inner voice. Those inner voices are your spiritual guides telling you what to do. Thoughts do not belong to you. Every thought you receive is given to you by a spirit including the spirits of déjà vu.

- When you receive a message from spirit, it will always be a helpful directive.
- Spirit guidance comes to you when it is necessary.
- Spirit guidance does not always come when you ask.
- Spirit guidance will help you when it is for the good all.
- Spirit guidance is not a haphazard spiritual energy.
- Your spiritual guidance is assigned to you specifically.

When you receive an instruction to do a thing, tell yourself the goal is to achieve. Allow yourself the indulgence to be spontaneous, and take action immediately. Allow yourself to be a freethinker, and tell yourself there are no mistakes. Be fearless at all times. Do your best to take advantage of every opportunity.

Revisit your embedded memories from time to time and perfect them in your mind. The spiritual realm gives you a memory to help you perfect yourself. Spirit will not waste its energy. When spirit delivers a message it expects you to act. The spirit of déjà vu expects you to be interested enough in your spiritual future to seek, and knock then the door will be opened. Most people do not take the time to figure out the message from déjà vu and loose an opportunity to receive greatly.

Your path is directed for you and deep within your beating heart you know this to be true. You are following the path of your destiny that has been assigned to you, and are given the ability to make choices along the way. How do you know if the action that you take is the right action? You do not know exactly which particular result your action will bring. Trust your future self, and listen to your inner energy.

Everything you will do brings you closer to your goal. It is not you but the Great Creative Substance that will declare when you have reached precision in a thing, and when you shall be done. Your heart will continue beating to the tune of its creator. You will continue to experience through awareness, recognition, and understanding.

Sincerity

Sincerity is a spirit, a separate and distinct personality, and it will join you after you have asked for it and when your energy vibrates to sincerities tune. You cannot give yourself sincerity. You must be sincere.

When I want to make friends with sincerity, I tell myself that this "thing," what ever it may be, is real. The power of belief is fundamental when asking the spirit of sincerity to join you. However, it is necessary for you to do more than believe. You must have a knowing. This knowing must vibrate deep down within your very being. This knowing makes a connection with sincerity and must never be allowed to fain. In your knowing, you will receive greatly, and you will receive sincerity.

At some point, you will re-connect with your true self. Some have already reconnected, but most are a narrow form of their true self serving through a personality. Until the true self is reconnected you do not know who you really are, you are guessing, and the spiritual realm knows more about you than you know about yourself. Sincerity is an absolute must. The spiritual realm is listening to you every second, of every minute, and it cannot be fooled.

Joy

You will create those things which bring you joy when you create with intention. We are explaining to you what joy is.

- When you experience something, and it makes you feel happy, once or repeatedly, that is joy.

Creating without intention brings, a haphazard, and messy lifestyle. Usually, those things that you would not want to experience over, and over again. Those things that will not bring you joy should be deleted from your thoughts.

Having immense joy in all that you do will bring you power, this power will make you strong, the strength you receive is a spirit that will help maintain your ability to receive your blessings.

Confidence

You shall know that the Great Creative Substance is real and this is all the confidence you need. Never tell yourself anything that is not going to help you win this time. First, it is not the winning against fellow patriarchs, beings of light, or humans on this earthly realm. The winning is against those energies that want you to stay stuck to the earthly habitat.

What is so important about winning? Beings of light have been travelling back and forth from other dimensions for, not thousands or million but billions of years. For thousands upon, thousands of years we have returned to this planet. The majority of us keep doing the same things over, and over again. Yes, most call it reincarnation. However, it is not necessary to believe in a life after death, to have the spark of truth ignited.

Every day you will give

the spirit of your mind direction.

-- G.H.J.R. The Anunnaki

THE SUBCONSCIOUS

Let us define what the subconscious mind is, as taught to me by my Spiritual Guidance G.H.J.R. The Anunnaki from Sirius. Here are the facts:

- The subconscious mind is not alone. It is accompanied by the soul, the conscious mind, and in my case the twin flame.

- The subconscious delivers the wisdom of the decree received from the soul to the conscious mind.

- The subconscious experiences awareness through the conscious mind.

- The sub conscious mind is a separate and distinct entity or personality from ourselves.

I found out something very spectacular here. The sub-conscious is a personality, and should be approached as such.

The Trinity

You ask who is the "we"? When we speak of the we it is the subconscious mind, the conscious mind, and the higher self.

Your higher self is not your guardian angel. The higher self is the same as the true self, which receives its instruction from the Most High. The true self is connected to the soul.

The soul releases the law and the decree of your experiences. The subconscious delivers the wisdom of the decree received from the soul to the conscious. The subconscious experiences awareness through the conscious. The conscious is the observer of everything you experience, and reports to the subconscious.

To receive your blessings, you will go through the helper whom abides with you, the subconscious. Christianity did not lie; they veiled it in a mystery. They told you to go through the son, to get to the father. They call it the holy trinity, the father, son, and Holy Spirit.

Father = Great Creative Substance

Son = True Self/Soul

Holy Spirit = Subconscious

You ask are there others helping? Yes, you have helpers and these helpers are strong and mighty. We are all with you, and we know your real and true vibratory energy. Until you become one with your true self we know better than you who, and what you truly are.

God's helpers are always listening and they are not in the physical realm. We speak to you through the wire (pineal). There are also other helpers assigned to you during this experience, and if allowed your Twin Flame will also become a helper. For the good of all, there may also be others in the spiritual realm allowed to experience through you.

Your true self is waiting for you to return. You will see us all again upon your return home. You are truly loved.

The Subconscious Is Gods Helper

Before asking god for anything scan your inner thoughts and intent know that you are sure about what you want. Speaking with Gods helpers is a serious act. When you ask, be sure that you want what you have asked. This helper is not a respecter of persons, and wants to please God. When you ask, be very sure that you want it! Tell God you want to learn how to take the free energy from Universal Source and use it to succeed.

This subconscious helper is with God, this helper will stay Gods helper. You will soon receive exactly what you asked. Be sure that it is what you want, this helper is sure that you will receive what you ask.

Then you will ask for what you want. You

will tell God what you want to experience. You will tell God while asking sincerely from your heart. You will tell God everything you want to receive, and you will believe you will.

The asking is for your benefit. The spirits within you hear you automatically, and will already know what you want and/or need. However, the asking is required, and it is not until you have asked that the request will be granted.

The helper knows that God has approved the request, and spoken to fulfill it. The helper knows that God is well pleased with the request, and the helper will be well pleased. The helper was created to bring you what you ask.

Be faithful in all things. The helper is willing to bring you everything that you ask for. The helper will tell God when you received it. The helper is a willing participant; the helper is a willing energy that has been assigned to your life experience. The helper is not God; the helper is energy sent by God, the helper is your subconscious mind. This helper thinks if you want this, you should have it. This helper will not bring you what you did not ask; this helper will bring you everything you ask.

Who is the Subconscious

The subconscious is a spirit with a unique and distinct personality. Everyone has a helper. This helper takes the energy from the Most High God and uses it freely to ensure you succeed this time.

- Your subconscious is a spirit, and has its own personality.
- Has been assigned to you by the Most High God.
- Is your helper.
- Has been told to listen to you constantly.
- Has been told to record every request.
- Has the ability to provide everything, and anything you ask for.
- Has the ability to do what earthly spirits cannot.

Face to Face With The Subconscious

How I met my subconscious mind. I am going to walk you through this particular spiritual meditation experience as it occurred.

This meditation journey starts off with me walking through a nature valley in the high peeks of a mountain. As I am walking through a trail surrounded by beautiful spring flowers in hues of yellow, pink, purple, blue and a combination of many other colors I have no particular thoughts on my mind just feeling good in the landscape as I observe the view. Yes, this place was not a thinking place, it was a feeling place. This is a different dimension, it is definitely not earth. Earth never felt this good, this relaxing, this calm. I love it.

Then in front of me a receptionist desk appeared. I find myself inside an immaculate room that was so large it had no walls, and this place was very professional yet magnificent and grand at the same time. On the other side of the desk was a man a young man, he could have been a boy, his age did not matter, it was his energy that stood out. He was not immature, his energy was extremely professional, approachable, caring but non personable. His style was sleek upbeat carefree no-nonsense with a penetrating intellect of insight and perception. He was definitely androgynous and more masculine than feminine. However, gender truly did not matter.

He was unlike any one I have ever met I admired him immensely and felt a closeness to him immediately. I did get the impression that my relationship with him can influence my earthly experiences. Still I had no idea where I was, or who he is. I am perplexed.

As soon as I entered he greeted me, and said go in. I stood there looking at him thinking to myself I like his style. A couple of times I looked past him into a magnificent room.

He sat in a chair and was slightly taller than me, in my standing position. His attitude told me that he does this all day everyday. It is his job he is a master of it, and he is extremely busy. He answers to a source higher than himself and a source higher than me. I am standing now directly in front of him. He was sitting at the desk doing some sort of work with his fingers. This place did not appear to be complex, yet it was completely above the power of my brain to conceptualize. The equipment he was working on seemed like some sort of computer.

Apparently, I was not ready to heed his direction to go in, and I was not afraid to speak to him because I asked "Where am I, what is this place?". We were not talking with our lips. I knew immediately everything he said without waiting to hear the sentences.

He didn't answer my questions instead he said "enter in." I stood there just peering past him, and needed more information before I entered in. I don't remember saying it but I was thinking it and he must have heard me because he told me again "enter in." I still stood there, and now I am asking questions. He did not answer my questions, and for the third time with a bit of annoyance he said "go in" and this time he added "ask for what ever you want and it will be given".

For some reason this answer completely satisfied me, and without another thought I immediately entered in.

Where Your True Self Resides

Immediately I was inside a gigantic enormous room. The room was wonderful, beautiful and everything that I would want to have if I lived in a magnificent castle. It was that type of room, and in front of me in this room was a really big pool. I stood there looking at the pool before entering into the room. The pool was right in the middle of everything and it was huge. I had to walk around the pool to view the space because it was in the middle of the room.

Just as I was about to make the turn around the pool I noticed someone standing there. I began to observe the person as I was walking, and saw that this person was me, and this room was her home. For some reason we did not speak to each other. We acknowledged each other, and moved together in unison but there was no conversation. It was as though this was naturally not yet the time and I kept moving around the pool with her following close behind and/or to the side of me.

On the other side of the pool now, and with my other self standing near me, I stopped to look out of an extremely large window. The most fabulous view I have ever seen went on for miles and it was all beautiful. In this space was everything that made me feel happy. There was nothing there that was unnecessary. I absolutely use water as a daily retreat, everything about the layout including the substances from which it was made (ex. marble, concrete etc.) gave me a certain feel that I like. As for the window view if I could look at it over and over again this would be the view that I would see.

This is the home that I am creating for myself in heaven from earth. My subconscious mind is watching it for me. He is the gatekeeper. Wow! It might sound a little ridiculous to you guys . . . but now, at least once per week I send flowers to my subconscious, and my true self to spruce the place up a little bit. I want them to be very comfortable.

One of the gifts I sent to my subconscious mind was a guard that towered above the front entrance. I sent the guard for the protection of my subconscious, and true self. Then, I received a message from my subconscious (he has a name but it is personal between him, and me so I will not mention it here) that the guard was awkward and I should send him back. Yes, I thought to myself that was a bit ridiculous they don't need protection.

I truly love my subconscious mind, and pray that we will be friends even after this life cycle. Thank you Great Omnipotent Heavenly Creator for every blessing. I am truly grateful for all of the help I receive.

I returned to full consciousness and asked my spiritual guidance about the experience. G.H.J.R. my heavenly guide explained that:

- I had just met my subconscious mind and the person that was with my sub conscious was my true self.

- I learned that my true self and my subconscious are together in the same space.
- My subconscious is a personality in another dimension, and although he seems human he is not.

I found out something very spectacular here. The sub-conscious is a distinct and separate personality, with feelings, and its own mind and should be approached as such.

Subconscious and True Self

Your Subconscious and your true self live together in the same space.

- Your Subconscious reports to your true self.
- Your Subconscious is not your guardian angel.
- Your Subconscious will make sure that God is well pleased.
- Your Subconscious will please God before pleasing you.
- Your Subconscious will stop at nothing to make sure your request is heard.

- Your Subconscious will give you exactly what you ask.

Best Friends

Become friends with the subconscious spirit. You must know that your subconscious believes in you, and will help you. Talk to your subconscious everyday, and become true friends. Be faithful, because you will truly receive. Your subconscious will help you immediately, and without question. In each moment, the answer to every question you have is given to you. Everyone is given a chance to realize his or her greatest victory and goal. Your subconscious will stop at nothing to make sure you receive.

Your subconscious has a name, and you should call it by name.

- Ask your subconscious mind to tell you what you should call it.
- Then you will listen for the name. Do not be concerned if you cannot hear at first.

Call your subconscious the first name that comes to mind after you ask.

- When you have a name, you will call it that name, even if you are in disbelief.

Your subconscious will change the name later if necessary. After the two of you have become friends and are listening to one another, you will be gratefully happy for the connection.

Help is always yours to receive. Help is always available to you. The Great Creative Substance is the ultimate omnipotent source of universal energy. From this great source of energy, all things are produced. We will not call this great creative substance a God because it is much more than that. Instead, we will describe it as the highest vibratory energy in existence.

Take the precious energy from Universal Source Energy and believe that you will succeed. You will take the energy from God that is given freely, and receive what you ask for.

- You will be successful when you are sincere.

- Do not take the precious energy that God gives so freely and destroy your chance to receive.

- God wants you to succeed.
- God wants you to believe that you will receive what you ask for.
- Tell God you want to use his energy for the good of all.

Energy is Given Freely

Tell Creative Source Energy/God how you feel. Tell Creative Source Energy that you want to be his best friend. Tell Creative Source Energy that you want to please him above all the worldly things that you have experienced in this life. Tell Creative Source Energy that you want to please God above all else. Tell Creative Source Energy you will wait to receive because you know you will receive on time. Tell Creative Source Energy you will wait to receive, and you will be pleased because you know the blessing will be exactly what you ask for.

Take Gods powerful energy, that is so freely given, and use it to succeed.

- Know, and be very sure that God wants you to succeed.
- Know that when you are successful you will truly please God.
- Know, and be very sure that when you please God you will truly be successful.
- Know that when God is satisfied, you will be satisfied.
- Know that when telling God you want anything, God is always pleased.

Things To Tell Your Creator

Be very sure, and know that God will provide you with your deepest desires, and wishes from your heart. This you must be sure of to succeed. Make Your Request the Anunnaki Way. So that you may succeed God will allow you to ask for what ever you desire.

Before asking here is a list of some things,

you may say to your creator.

Give thanks before asking for anything.

- You will thank God at all times, and before you ask of God, you will thank him first.

- You will make your request, and you will not demand.

- You will believe that God is your friend.

- You will tell God that you belong to him and him only.

- You will tell God that you ask because God is truly all that you really have.

- You will tell God everything that you want.

- You will tell God that you want to succeed, and you want to be helped now.

- You will tell God that you want these things so that you will succeed, and so that God will be truly pleased.

- You will tell God that you need these things to succeed in this earthly realm.

  Tell God you need these things so that when

you return to him, he will be well pleased. Tell God that he will only be well pleased if he sends you help.

"The more you concentrate on a thing, the more it concentrates on you."

-- G.H.J.R. The Anunnaki

FOUR STEPS TO REPROGRAM THE SUBCONSCIOUS

The method given here to communicate with your subconscious spirit is the same method that Psychic Spirit Fairie uses to speak with, and to garner her subconscious power daily. The directives for this communication technique came channeled from, G.H.J.R. The Anunnaki King of Nibiru, and Universal Energy.

For me receiving signals from the subconscious was a work in progress and I progressed in direct correspondence to the amount of work I put in. The moment I knew without a doubt that my subconscious was a real spirit person with a separate and distinct personality, with feelings, we became friends immediately. However, receiving specifically requested signals took a little longer, and depending upon the request I gave, it took anywhere from approximately 10-60 days. Everyday at the same time (during my morning walks), I made the request until I received. I no longer have to ask, and I continue to receive to this day, more than two years later.

My received results from the subconscious spirit are in direct and exact answer to my request. I requested to receive a signal and that this signal will be delivered to me as a warning to change a thought or action that is not beneficial to my present or future success. I received exactly what I asked.

It does not have to, and will not take years to get your subconscious mind to listen to you. This is a four step process that your subconscious will obey. Within the process are proven methods that quickly motivate your subconscious spirit. This process takes at the most 8 weeks depending upon your persistence it could be much quicker. Using this method of communication with your subconscious mind will help you receive everything you want.

Believe me this works. Using this technique is how I got my subconscious mind to listen to me. Whenever I am receiving a wrong thought, or about to make a mistake, I receive a warning signal. This signal manifests noticeably without pain, in the same place each time. Now it is almost impossible for me to make a mistake.

The following are the exact steps my spirit guide G.H.J.R. gave me. These steps have proven to be proficient in reprogramming the subconscious spirit. These steps reprogrammed the spirit of my subconscious mind quickly and accurately. Give it a try and let the process work for you. This practice works quickly and brings results that work. Praise God for his many blessings. You can use these steps for any area of your life.

STEP ONE

- Speak to this subconscious personality as though it is a person.

Now you call this power your subconscious mind. Soon you will have become best friends with this power, and call it by name.

STEP TWO

- Give this subconscious power a name.
- When speaking with this power you will not kick it around, demand, or give it orders.
- Treat this spirit with the utmost respect or it will not listen to you.
- Do not upset this spirit. If you treat this spirit with unkindness, it will tell the creator that you are not ready to receive. Your wait may be much longer if this happens.
- The subconscious spirit answers to God and not you. In other words, you are not its boss. The Universal Creative Substance controls the subconscious, and not you.

Convince the Subconscious

The only way you can get the subconscious spirit to help you is if it believes you. The subconscious mind is a pure, trusting spirit and will believe anything you tell it over, and over again. This spirit will take a record of how many times you have repeated yourself. Your determination will be seen as a symbol of your sincerity.

- Gentle commands will reprogram this spirit.

STEP THREE

Command the subconscious.

Say:

1. Subconscious (call the spirit by name) you will do the request and you have five minutes to respond.
2. Subconscious (call the spirit by name) you will send a sign that the request has been done.
3. You will send the same sign each time, and in the same place, and this sign will not hurt.

4. Subconscious (call the spirit by name) every time you deliver a blessing you will receive a blessing.

5. Subconscious (call the spirit by name) every time you listen you will truly receive greatly, and our God will be proud.

6. Be blessed Subconscious (call the spirit by name). Now go and do it. You have five minutes to complete my request, or five minutes to respond and tell me that you are working on it.

7. Subconscious (call the spirit by name) if I do not get a response from you I will tell The Most High God that you are not listening. God will not be pleased with this news.

8. You will want God to be pleased in all things.

9. Listen to me you have five minutes to respond. Go quickly now IAM waiting.

Your Subconscious Listened

After receiving the requested signal from your subconscious, thank the Great Creative

Substance for giving you help in the form of your subconscious mind. Then tell your subconscious the following:

STEP FOUR

- Tell your subconscious mind/helper you may stop sending me the signal now.
- When I receive my blessing, you will be blessed also.
- I will tell The Most High God you listened to me.

Your Subconscious Did Not Listen

Did Your Subconscious Ignore You? It is a requirement that you ask again. You must teach your subconscious to listen. Try this if you did not receive a response.

Be firm.

Say:

- I gave you a directive.
- Then gave you five minutes to respond.

- Subconscious mind you will truly listen to me this is my vessel and IAM the boss.

Although you will be firm, you will also be kind. Remember the subconscious is connected to your conscious, and lives in the same space as your true self. Therefore, you are also speaking to yourself. Love yourself and be kind. There is no need to be angry. Additionally, your subconscious is no push over, and is extremely intelligent.

1. I will tell you again go and get the request done, and get it done quickly.
2. You have five minutes to respond.
3. When it is done you will send a sign, and this sign that you send, will be the same sign every time.
4. After I receive your response I will tell the Most High God that you listened to me.
5. After I receive my blessing, I will thank the Most High God for blessing me, and ask that you be blessed also.

6. I must receive a response from thee, or this
    time I will truly tell the Most High God and
    he will not be pleased.

Then you will wait five (5) minutes. You
will either get a response, sent as a body signal or
some other outwardly sign, or you will get nothing.

Removing Resistance

Scan yourself completely for a sign, any sort
of sign. If you are certain that you have not
received an answer it could be that your
subconscious helper is not taking you seriously.
Perhaps your command is not obeyed because this
spirit helper does not believe in you, or because it
never had to listen to you before therefore it is not
in a rush to listen to you now.

There could be another reason why your
subconscious did not listen. Perhaps you have some
resistance to the request. Ask again, be humble and
listen for any resistance. If there is resistance
switch it and give your subconscious mind a reason
to believe that what you are asking for will succeed,

and why you should receive. If you can give your subconscious a reason to believe that this request will work, it is because you believe it also. If you do not believe you must work on yourself until you do believe. The subconscious listens for sincerity.

Your subconscious resides with your true self and knows more about you than you know about yourself. Your subconscious is listening and hears everything. It shall not be fooled, it will report to the creator everything in truth. Remember the subconscious is dedicated to pleasing God above everything. You must be sincere!

Your subconscious will not help you unless you can find a reason for this thing to become a possibility. If you are having difficulty believing here is something you can do every night before retiring.

Affirm: "The rule is there are no rules IAM receiving the request now. Subconscious what is my next step."

After affirming this every night for some time you will receive an answer. (depending on your relationship with your subconscious).

If you find no resistance within yourself then your subconscious must listen. You must make your subconscious believe it has no choice, other than listen to you. This is your vessel and insolence will not be allowed. It is time to stop being Mr. or Ms. Nice Guy. Stop talking to your subconscious altogether. Your creator is the true boss of you both. You should not be in the bosses office everyday. Nevertheless, it is now time to go straight to God, and tell God everything. Your subconscious will not like it

Say:

"Heavenly Great Omnipotent Source of All I gave my subconscious a directive and my subconscious did not listen to me. I need my subconscious to listen, and my subconscious (call it by name) must listen to me if I am going to truly receive. I want to win this time. Tell my subconscious (call it by name) to listen to me, and tell my subconscious to do everything I tell it to do. I need help I cannot do this alone. Thank you Great Divine Director, you are my source for everything and you will truly be pleased with me."

At this point you should be receiving some definite signs. The subconscious wants you to know it is trying. Always be kind to your subconscious because this spirit is probably sending you a sign that is too weak for you to notice. You must train your subconscious, and you must be alert. Pay attention to the signs. A finger might jump an itch that does not go away. Accept the signs even if they arrive in an unprecedented place.

If you receive any sort of sign thank your subconscious, and then remind this spirit how you want to receive the sign. Give constant reminders until it happens.

The Last Alternative

Still Nothing? When your subconscious does not listen, you must not give up. You must keep working at it until it does listen. Your subconscious received a command from The Most Omnipotent Source of All Things to listen to you. Your subconscious must listen to you or face the possibility of replacement.

Reasons why your subconscious does not listen to you are because it does not believe you, or is accustomed to doing whatever it wants. You must be firm and make the subconscious believe that you are taking over, and now it must listen.

You cannot live this life without the subconscious mind it is the helper that delivers what you need. The more persistent you are the more you will receive. You will continue to converse with the spirit of your subconscious until it obeys you.

Your subconscious can be replaced. However, this spirit will not be replaced without serious detriment to your soul. Remember that your soul is your true self, and it resides in the same space as your subconscious. They live together in the same house.

The last alternative is to ask for the subconscious spirit to be replaced. It should never be necessary. Your holy guardian angel will get involved before you have to ask for another subconscious spirit. Your subconscious mind may be stubborn, but it will eventually listen. The good news is that your subconscious spirit friend will never stop listening to you once it begins.

Your subconscious spirit will never become your enemy. Be faithful everything your subconscious does is with the permission of its creator. The subconscious is always watching its back, or making sure that it does not get into any trouble with The Great Creative Substance which formed it. Your last recourse is to ask God to replace your subconscious spirit helper.

You will not be happy if your subconscious should become discouraged. Do not play with your subconscious mind. Your subconscious maintains its happiness at all times, and will not want to listen to you if you have a bad attitude. If you do have a dependable bad attitude spirit following you constantly you will be blocked by the subconscious mind. Make sure your subconscious spirit remains happy. Maintain the spirit of joy and your subconscious will reward you. If you have not yet swallowed the red pill then you are not re-connected to your true self. And what is the red pill, it is the emergency button you must push for the constant mental and physical agility needed to sustain your efforts. Persuade yourself to stay happy.

Your subconscious mind is serious about pleasing God, and knows what you are thinking, before you consciously know what you are thinking. It never stops listening to you. This spirit is very good at its job, and executes it flawlessly.

Say very lovingly:

"Heavenly Great Omnipotent Source of All. I gave my subconscious many directives and my subconscious did not listen to me. I need my my subconscious (call it by name) to listen to me, love me, and be my friend. I want to win this time and return home to you happy, having fulfilled my mission completely. I cannot do it alone, I rely on you alone. Creator of All Heavenly Great Omnipotent Source if my subconscious will refuse to answer me I ask for a subconscious that will. Tarry not Father IAM desperate for help Now! Winning is a requirement for me I will accept nothing less. Replace that which is not fulfilling my destiny. I must have a subconscious that listens to me. Thank you Great Divine Director, you are my source for everything and you will truly be pleased with me."

Consciously Accept This

- God has assigned to you a helper.

- The helper listens to every request.

- Before God sends your blessing the helper will report to God exactly what you have said.

- There is always a witness to everything that you say and do.

- The helper delivers your blessings.

- The helper is able to give you whatever you ask.

- The helper brings you exactly what you ask for.

- The helper is able to do what you ask, when the otherworldly spirits cannot.

The Great IAM gives to you freely all the energy you will need to manifest your will. When you ask for help, you will receive, each time you act with purpose you will gain an opportunity to create with accuracy.

The Helper Is Not Your Savior

You are your only savior. It is your responsibility to save yourself or you will lose the energy you have been given for this life journey, and need to return. You will not be allowed into the kingdom that created you until your soul has experienced what it set out to experience and re-purifies itself. This spirit helper of the subconscious mind is your friend, and along with all of the other spirit helpers in spiritual realms are guiding you through your earthly sojourn. You shall be your own savior through the use of your will.

- The helper is with you because God told him to.
- This helper is a friend to your soul.
- This helper is with you until the end.
- This helper is with you through it all.
- This helper will never leave you.
- This helper wants to be with you, wants to make sure that you know God is with you until the end of time.

The Delivery of Your Request

Your exact request is given to you when you trust, and you are sincere. Although you have not seen these things yet you will trust that you will receive them. It will be in your best interest to walk by faith, until you live by sight.

Say: "I will walk by faith, till I live by sight."

When you receive from God the Anunnaki way your requests are delivered in accordance with your own faith, and trust. When you receive your delivered request you have truly been blessed. You will tell everyone you meet that you received the Anunnaki way.

As soon as you have gotten the answer and/or the delivery of your request:

- Tell God that your request has just been delivered to you.
- Tell God, that what you received is, exactly what you requested.

You will receive after you have requested with sincerity, trusted that God heard your request, and had faith that your exact request shall be delivered by Universal Energy. Ask daily because you will wait (this depends on your relationship with your spirits within).

When this helper brings the blessing you asked for, he will tell God that you have accepted it. Then God will thank the helper, and tell the helper to listen for your next request. The helper listens constantly to hear your request. The helper will stop at nothing to ensure he/she hears every request. The helper wants to please God above all else. The helper is bringing your blessings from God to help you through the life experience.

Chronicles of the Subconscious

This is a brief story of an experience I had with my subconscious. I awoke to a male voice that was not my spiritual guide G.H.J.R. The voice had a busy, although not rushed sound to it. The voice asked me in what manner I wanted to experience an event. My first thought was to please the other party concerned. As soon as that thought entered my mind, the voice said "be true to yourself, what do you really want to experience."

After searching my soul, which only took seconds, I replied with my answer. "All right" I heard the voice say, and within milliseconds, I heard a ticker tape noise, kind of like a computer zipping. Then the voice and its presence were gone.

"That is it, that was my subconscious mind. That is how my subconscious hears, answers, and delivers." I shall be true to myself at all times.

"Wish the best for those that do not wish the same for you. In this way they will become an obstacle for themselves. When you wish good for those that do not wish good for you. They become Gods problem and not an obstacle for you."

-- G.H.J.R. The Anunnaki

CONCLUSION

When People Want You To Fail

God wants you to succeed. Here is how to succeed when others want you to fail.

When you tell God that you love him, and want to please him you will succeed, the Anunnaki way. You will find that heavenly hosts hear every prayer.

- You will thank God before you receive the things you ask for.

God will hear you, and send everything that you ask.

- Tell God you want these things fast and in a hurry.

- Tell God you will stop asking after you receive it.
- Tell God you will keep asking until you get it.
- Tell God that you will continue asking until you receive, because you wait to receive, and you want to receive everyday, that is why you will keep asking.
- Tell God you know he heard you, and you want to believe so you will keep asking.

Now, ask God to tell those people that matter to you the most that you want to succeed, and you will succeed if they believe it to. Meditate on these things and your creator will be sure to help you.

- Tell God you need people to believe with you to succeed.
- Tell God what you need to help you succeed, and tell God you want it fast.
- Tell God to tell those people you will receive quickly if they believe too.

- Tell God you want to be successful, and with the help of God, it will happen quickly.
- Tell God you are his creation, and to please help you.

Now tell yourself you will do all things, and everything to please God. Your life, soul, and complete being are receiving blessings at all times, now tell yourself, that you are blessed, and you will be. We are the Anunnaki.

Consider These Things

- Intellect is a helper and a servant to the spirit.
- Physical body is vessel and servant for the spirit.
- Before the creation of your body, your spirit existed, in a pure, untarnished, and unadulterated state of existence holding no falsehood.
- This earth needs your unique energy to help keep it prosperous, and it keeps you going around in circles. Without your energy,

everything on this planet would be useless.

Individual thought forms, and energies are different and unique because of the connected energy.

- Everyone has created their reality on earth through their mind.
- Spirit is the life force and without it your body is nothing.
- There is a spirit behind every thought and emotion in existence.

You will make your request known to God. Your voice will be heard when you are sincere. You receive an answer when you trust. The answer will be a witness, and proof that God is real. Your faith gets stronger every time you receive a blessing and the Universe is a witness of your belief.

A Message from G.H.J.R. The Anunnaki

That is why we are telling you the truth, because we want to help you. The truth is we will talk to God for you. We will be your helper, if you ask us to. The truth is that God wants to have you succeed, and God wants you to win. God created you, and will take care of you forever; God is willing to do anything to help you.

You do not receive help because you do this or do that in any special way, or that you did anything to deserve it. You do not receive help because you personally asked and God likes you more than the other. You ask for your benefit. Not for the benefit of your Creator, but for the benefit of yourself. God is always there whether you ask or not. God wants you to win, and we want you to succeed. Take care, and be blessed.

About The Author

Kaciana Bru is a spiritualist, empirical with no prejudices, idols, or religious beliefs. Love, and freedom are her beliefs, and the highest infinite life force is her god. Ms. Bru is a contemporary spiritual teacher primarily dedicated to the saturation of the highest formula of wisdom.

Kaciana Bru, Psychic Spirit Fairie is a world traveller having received extensive spiritual guidance in her travels through Cypress, England, France, Greece, Israel, Russia, Italy, Mexico, Roma, Bahamas, Canada, Costa Rica and more.

Experience a higher level of guidance and understanding with this sincere, honest, and kind psychic of integrity. Be prepared to experience your dreams with this life changing spiritual guide. A three-time book author, and highly recognized as a Master Psychic for all areas of psychic spirituality.

There is an awakening sweeping over the entire earth that no man can stop. More people are coming to realize that the true spirit of god is within each and every individual. People use to believe spirituality is located through participation in a religion or organized system of beliefs. We are establishing new beliefs. Spirituality is not a link to religion; it is a link to your inner self. Your true religion is your dedication to The Great Omnipotent Source of All Things (God), and the promotion of the power within.

Commanding The Spirits Within.

Use your powerful temple

of vibrating energy to win.

Made in United States
North Haven, CT
02 March 2022

16719880R00065